Glamourista

Jennifer Zimmermann

Glamourista: An Adult Coloring Book of Fashion, Jewels and Beauty

Copyright © 2016 Jennifer Zimmermann. All rights reserved.

Cover and Interior Design: Jennifer Zimmermann

ISBN-10: 0-692-81116-8
ISBN-13: 978-0-692-81116-0

You can find me here:

Sign up for Jennifer's newletter to receive occasional freebies and stay up to date, at
ModernColoring.com

Coloring Tips: www.moderncoloring.com/tips-tricks

Want to learn how to color gems and other advanced techniques?

Watch Jennifer's tutorials on YouTube:
www.youtube.com/channel/UC0Rwvht-rHECPDwiNj4gP7w

Facebook Artist Page: Modern Coloring: Jennifer Zimmermann
www.facebook.com/moderncoloring/

Instagram: www.instagram.com/moderncoloring/

Pinterest: www.pinterest.com/moderncoloring/

Twitter: twitter.com/moderncoloring

Amazon Author Page: www.amazon.com/-/e/B01GNGL18Y

For a limited time, enjoy bonus digital downloads that accompany this book on ModernColoring.com!
You can find your exclusive download code printed on the backside one of the last pages of your book.

<u>Please</u> don't forget to leave a review of *Glamourista*! It is very much appreciated.

Special thanks to my beautiful models, fabulous creative team and brilliant advisors:

LoLo, Amy, Mel, Bella, Ban, Shoo, Matt, Anne, and Arnie

I couldn't have done this without the encouragement of my wonderful family.
I am ever grateful for the endless patience and support of my husband and kids.

I am beyond appreciative of my loyal colorists and love seeing them share all of their amazing
creations and I cannot wait to see what they do with these illustrations! :)

Happy coloring!

-Jennifer

This Book Belongs To:

Heather Wells

Colorist: _____   ___/___/___

Colorist: _____ ___/___/___

Colorist: _____   ___/___/___

Colorist: _____ ___/___/___

Colorist: _____ ___/___/___

Colorist: _____ ___/___/___

Colorist: _____ _____ / _____ / _____

Colorist: _____ ____ / / ____

Colorist: _____ ____/____/____

Colorist: _____ ___/___/___

Colorist: _____ ___/___/___

Colorist: _____   ___/___/___

Colorist: _____ ____/__/__

Colorist: _____ ___/___/___

Colorist: _____ ___/___/___

Colorist: _____ ___/___/___

Colorist: _____ ___/___/___

Colorist: _____ ___/___/___

Colorist: _____ ____/____/____

Colorist: _____ ___/___/___

Colorist: _____ ___ / / ___

Colorist: _____

Colorist: _____ ___/___/___

Colorist: _____ ____/____/____

Colorist:_____   ___/___/___

Colorist: _____

Colorist: _____ ___/___/___

Colorist: _____ ___/___/___

Colorist: _____ ___/___/___

Colorist: _____ ____ / / ____

Colorist: _____

Colorist: _____ ___/___/___

Colorist: _____ ____ / ___ /

Colorist: _____

Colorist: _____ ___/___/___

Colorist: _____

Colorist: _____ ___/___/___

Colorist: _____ ___ / / ___

Colorist:_____

Colorist:_____ ___/ /___

Colorist: _____ ____/____/____

Colorist: _____ ____ / / ____

Colorist: _____

Colorist: _____   __/__/__

Colorist: _____ ___ / ___ / ___

Colorist: _____

Colorist: _____ ____/ /____

Colorist: _____

Colorist: _____ ___/___/___

Colorist: _____ ___/___/___

Colorist: _____ ____/____/____

Colorist: _____

Colorist: _____

Glamourista

Colorist: _____ ____/____/____

Colorist: _____ ___ / ___ / ___

Colorist: _____ ___/___/___

Colorist: _____   ____/____/____   Code: VIP

40051407R00062

Made in the USA
Middletown, DE
01 February 2017